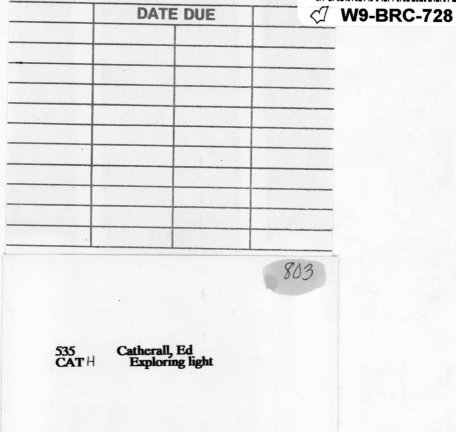

	DATE DUE		

Exploring Science

The Exploring Science series is designed to familiarize young students with science topics taught in grades 4–9. The topics in each book are divided into knowledge and understanding sections, followed by exploration by means of simple projects or experiments. The topics are also sequenced from easiest to more complex, and should be worked through until the correct level of attainment for the age and ability of the student is reached. Carefully planned Test Yourself questions at the end of each topic allow the student to gain a sense of achievement on mastering the subject.

EXPLORING
LIGHT

Ed Catherall

STECK-VAUGHN
LIBRARY
Austin, Texas

Exploring Science

Electricity
Magnets
Light
Soil
Sound
Weather

Cover illustrations:
Left *A double rainbow over Arizona.*
Above right *The lights of Manhattan at night.*
Below right *A spectrum formed by refraction of light through a prism.*

Frontispiece *A spectacular display of Christmas tree lights at Grand Army Plaza, New York.*

Editor: Elizabeth Spiers
Editor, American Edition: Susan Wilson
Series designer: Ross George

Published in the United States in 1990 by Steck–Vaughn Co., Austin, Texas, a subsidiary of the National Education Corporation.

First published in 1989 by
Wayland (Publishers) Ltd

©Copyright 1989 Wayland (Publishers) Ltd

Library of Congress Cataloging-in-Publication Data

Catherall, Ed.
  Exploring light / Ed Catherall.

    p. cm.—(Exploring science)
  "First published in 1989 by Wayland (Publishers) Ltd.—T.p. verso
    Includes bibliographical references.
    Summary: Text, projects, and experiments explore light
sources, rainbows, color and light, reflections, prisms, optical illusions,
and other aspects of light.
    ISBN 0-8114-2591-6
    1. Light—Juvenile literature. 2. Light—Experiments—Juvenile
literature. [1. Light, 2. Light—Experiments. 3. Experiments.]
  I. Title. II. Series: Catherall, Ed. Exploring science.
  QC360.C37 1990   69-28063
  535—dc20   CIP
                                                                    AC
Printed in Italy by G. Canale, C.S.p.A., Turin
Bound in the United States
1 2 3 4 5 6 7 8 9 0 GC 94 93 92 91 90

Contents

LIGHT SOURCES

Light is vital to us. It is a form of energy, like heat and sound. Light helps us see our surroundings. The sun is our most important source of light and provides light energy to plants. If the sun were to go out, all living things on earth would soon die and our planet would be lifeless and frozen. There are other suns in the sky, but they are so far away that we call them stars. On a clear night, thousands of stars can be seen as small sources of light. We often describe light by how it is made. Sunlight, moonlight, and starlight are examples of natural light. Artificial light is made by humans—some examples are electric light, neon light, gaslight, candlelight, and firelight. These artificial lights enable humans to work at night and add to natural lighting during the day. For us to be able to see, the light must travel from the light source and enter our eyes. Here, it makes signals that are sent to the brain. These signals are interpreted by the brain and as a result we see images.

Sunset over Lake Baringo in Kenya. Without the sun's light energy, we would not exist and our planet would be a lifeless rock.

ACTIVITY

HOW LIGHT TRAVELS

YOU NEED

- **3 cards**
- **a hole puncher**
- **some thread or string**
- **modeling clay**
- **a flashlight**

WARNING: Looking directly at the sun or a strong light can hurt your eyes.

1 Make a hole in the middle of each card.
2 Use lumps of clay to hold the cards in an upright position on a table.
3 Line up the cards so that all the holes are in a straight line. Check this by passing a length of thread or string through the holes.

4 Remove the string. Can you see through the three holes?
5 Darken the room. Ask a friend to shine the flashlight through the first hole.

6 Where does the ray of light fall?
7 Move one of the cards about an inch to the left. What happens to the ray of light now?

Notice that the light from a source, such as your flashlight, can travel only in a straight line.

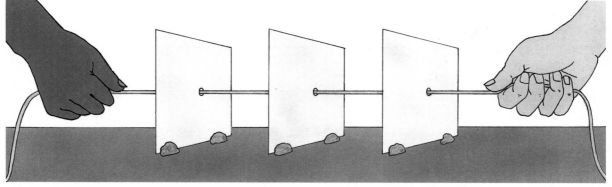

TEST YOURSELF

1. What is our most important light source?
2. Make a list of things that give light.
3. Name a light source that gives out heat as well as light.
4. How does light travel?

LIGHT AND DARK

A landscape in Germany in winter and summer. The shadows are longer in winter, when the sun is lower.

Light travels in straight lines. If you put an opaque object in the path of a beam of light, a shadow is made because light cannot shine through the object. It is dark on the other side of the object. Opaque objects cast clear, dark shadows. The earth is an opaque object. The sun shines on one side and it is day. The other side is in shadow and it is night. The earth spins from west to east, making one whole turn every 24 hours. This is why the sun seems to move across the sky. Night falls as the earth spins around and the sun disappears over the horizon.

The earth is tilted at an angle to the sun. In winter, the earth tilts away from the sun on our half of the planet. On the other half of the world, it is summer, because the earth is tilted toward the sun.

Before clocks were invented, people used the position of the sun to tell the time. They realized that shadows move as the sun moves and were able to invent a simple sundial—the shadow stick.

ACTIVITIES

SHADOWS

YOU NEED

- **cellophane tape**
- **a large sheet of white paper**
- **modeling clay**
- **a flashlight**
- **a pencil**

1 Put a table against the wall. Tape a sheet of white paper to the wall just above the table.
2 Use modeling clay to stand a pencil upright on the table.
3 Shine a flashlight from the edge of the table to the wall.
4 Darken the room. Look at the shadow.
5 Move the flashlight from side to side to see how the shadow moves.

6 Move the flashlight nearer to the pencil. What happens?

7 Take the paper off the wall and tape it to the tabletop.

8 Using modeling clay stand the pencil upright in the middle of the paper.

9 Shine the flashlight from above.

10 Get a friend to draw the position of the shadow.

11 Move the flashlight to a new spot. How does the shadow change?

12 Draw the position of the new shadow. Do your experiment a few more times.

SHADOW STICKS

> **YOU NEED**
>
> - **a sunny day**
> - **a long, straight stick**
> - **6 small sticks with labels**
> - **a ruler**
> - **a protractor**

1 Place the long stick upright in the ground.

2 Mark the position of the shadow every hour with a small stick.

3 Write the time on the label.

4 Measure the length of each shadow formed by the long stick.

5 Measure the angle between each shadow, using the protractor.

6 Draw your shadows to scale (e.g. one inch to ten inches).

The earth rotates completely every day. One complete turn is 360° in 24 hours. This means that the earth rotates 15° every hour. Check your sundial measurements. Were you correct?

TEST YOURSELF

1. Draw a picture including the sun in the sky. Show the positions of the shadows from the objects in the picture.

2. At which time of the year would the shadows from your shadow stick be the longest? Explain your answer.

LIGHT THROUGH THINGS

The lenses of sunglasses are made from translucent plastic or glass. Some of the light passes through, so that the man can see clearly. The rest is scattered by the lenses.

You know (from page 8) that if you put an opaque object in the path of a beam of light, that object will cast a clear, dark shadow. The light does not go through the opaque object, but bounces off its surface and scatters. The scattered light enters our eyes and we can see the object.

If the object is transparent, all the light will pass through it and no light will be scattered off its surface. The best known transparent substances are pure air, pure water, and pure glass. However, two of these are not completely transparent, as there is some light-scattering in water and in glass. That is why we can see them. A really transparent object would be invisible, and would cast no shadow.

Many objects are translucent, which means that they will let some light through. There will also be much light scattering from the surface. Because of this, translucent objects are useful as lamp shades and sunglasses. These objects cut out the glare of bright light, while allowing you to see through them. They cast fuzzy, pale shadows. You can use a light meter to find out how much light passes through translucent objects. Clouds are translucent, which is why the sun's light can pass through them. Because clouds are translucent, shadows are not easily seen on cloudy days. If clouds were opaque, it would be as dark as night when clouds were in front of the sun.

ACTIVITY

YOU NEED

- a variety of objects, including leaves and petals
- a flashlight
- a variety of glass and plastic bottles
- a drinking glass
- an assortment of liquids such as water, detergent, cooking oil, and bubble bath
- different kinds of paper

1 Get a friend to hold a flashlight close to each solid object.

2 Look at each from the other side.

3 Record whether the object is opaque, transparent, or translucent. What type of shadow does it cast?

4 Hold the flashlight close to each glass or plastic bottle. Select the one that is most transparent.

5 Check the drinking glass. Does it cast a shadow? Is it transparent? Put water in it. How transparent is it now?

6 Record how translucent each kind of paper is and arrange the paper in order. Put a spot of water and a spot of oil on each piece of paper.

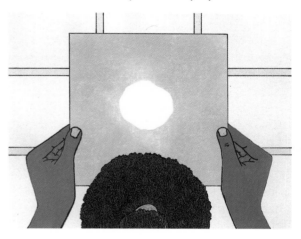

7 Hold the paper up to the light. What happens to the light shining through? What makes the paper more translucent—oil or water?

TEST YOURSELF

1. Are you opaque, transparent, or translucent?

2. List three opaque, three transparent, and three translucent things.

3. What happens to light shining on a sheet of paper soaked with oil?

4. Describe one use for translucent materials.

RAINBOWS

You know that pure water and pure glass are almost transparent. They let most of the light shine through, but just enough light is scattered and changed to enable us to see the water and glass (see page 10). However, if sunlight or white light shines on transparent water or glass at an angle, the light is broken up into colors. Each of these colors is colored light.

When sunlight shines on falling raindrops, the light is split up into the colors of the rainbow, as it passes through each raindrop. Usually, a single rainbow is seen, but occasionally there will be two rainbows (a double rainbow). The rainbow's colors are in an arranged order called the light spectrum. If sunlight or white light strikes glass at an angle, the light can be split into the colors of the spectrum.

Sir Isaac Newton was the first person to use a prism to split white light into its spectrum colors. Newton used a second prism to collect the spectrum colors, making them join to form white light again.

A double rainbow. The second, fainter one, always has its colors reversed.

ACTIVITIES

MAKING RAINBOWS

YOU NEED
- **a sunny day**
- **a clear drinking glass**
- **water**
- **a sheet of white paper**
- **crayons or colored pencils**
- **books**
- **a large prism**
- **a strong flashlight or slide projector**

WARNING: Never look directly at the sun.

1 Place a drinking glass of water on a window sill in direct sunlight.
2 Fill the glass to the brim with water.
3 Find the rainbow made on the floor.

4 Place a sheet of white paper where the rainbow falls.
5 Make a record of the rainbow with crayons or colored pencils.

MAKING A SPECTRUM

1 Put the prism on its side on the top of a pile of books.
2 Darken the room. Switch on the flashlight or slide projector.

4 Slowly turn and move the prism until a clear spectrum is formed on the wall.
5 Identify the colors. Are they the same as the other spectrum?

3 Move the prism so that light from the flashlight or slide projector will shine through it.

6 You can also look for a spectrum when light strikes the sloping edges of mirrors.

TEST YOURSELF

1. Which colors make white light?
2. How are rainbows made?
3. List three places where you might see a spectrum.

COLOR AND LIGHT

You can see an opaque object because light is scattered off its surface and enters your eyes (see page 10). Humans, birds, and certain other animals can see color. A blue car looks blue in white light because it scatters blue light from its surface. It absorbs all the other colors found in white light. Similarly, a yellow dress looks yellow in white light because it scatters yellow light from its surface and absorbs all the other colors that make up white light. However, if white light is shone onto a dull, black piece of coal, all the colors that make up white light are absorbed into the surface of the chunk of coal.

This Malaysian horned frog is a perfect example of animal camouflage. It is colored to resemble the leaves it sits on.

We see a black object mainly because it is against a lighter background. A black object against a black background is difficult to see, because very little light is scattered. Some animals have coloring similar to their surroundings. This blending into the background is called camouflage. An animal that is camouflaged is often spotted or striped, and keeps away from strong light. Spots and stripes make the shape of an animal hard to see from a distance.

ACTIVITIES

CAMOUFLAGE

YOU NEED

- **white paper**
- **colored paper**
- **scissors**
- **paint and paintbrush**

1 Cut out different fish shapes.

2 Paint each fish with stripes or spots.
3 Use different size stripes and spots.
4 Use a slightly different color for each fish.
5 Paint sheets of paper with backgrounds that match each fish.
6 Which fish is best camouflaged?
7 What happens if you use different colored paper for the background?
8 Collect animal camouflage pictures.

WARNING COLORS

Many animals display warning colors. Warning colors are the opposite of camouflage. These animals are avoided when they are seen. Some harmless animals have warning colors which make them look like creatures that taste unpleasant or are dangerous. We use warning colors to show danger, or to tell others to avoid us.

This poisondart frog, which lives in the rain forest of Guyana, has brightly colored skin to warn other creatures that it is poisonous.

1 Find pictures of animals having warning colors, and try to find out what they are imitating.
2 Look for warning colors in posters and traffic signs. Are there any particular colors that are used?
3 Design a poster using warning colors.

TEST YOURSELF

1. Why does a white car look white in white light?
2. Why does a red chair look red in white light? Can you determine what colors have been absorbed by the chair?
3. List three animals with camouflage and three that have warning colors.

COLORED LIGHT

You know what happens when white light shines onto different objects. The rules change though when the light is colored.

If you shine red light onto a red dress, for example, all the red light is scattered from the dress, that looks red. If you shine blue light onto that red dress, all the blue light will be absorbed. The dress will look black, because no light will be reflected. A colored filter, such as colored cellophane, will only let one color through. If you shine white light onto a red filter, only red will pass through. The filter absorbs all the other spectrum colors. You could say that a pure red filter is opaque to green and blue light. It is transparent only to red. Mixing colored lights is different from mixing colored paints. For example, shining red and green light together gives yellow light. If you add blue light to yellow light, you get white light. The primary colors of the light spectrum are red, green, and blue. They join together to make white light. Compare this with the primary colors of paints. These are red, blue, and yellow. They mix to make dark brown.

Above *The primary colors of light (left) and paints (right).*

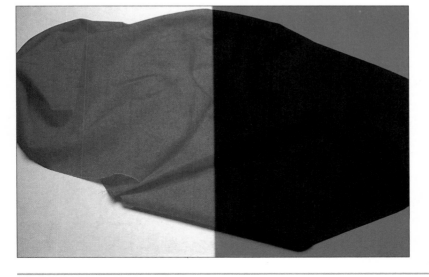

Left *All the red light scattered from the surface of this cloth is absorbed by the green filter. No light reaches the film in the camera.*

ACTIVITIES

LOOKING THROUGH COLORED FILTERS

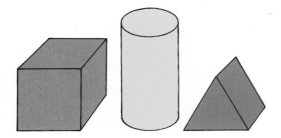

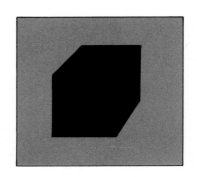

1 Look at the colored objects without using a filter.
2 Record the colors.

3 Look at the objects again through one of your colored filters.
4 What colors do they seem to be now?
5 Repeat the experiment, using each colored filter.
6 Record your results.

MAKING A COLOR BOX

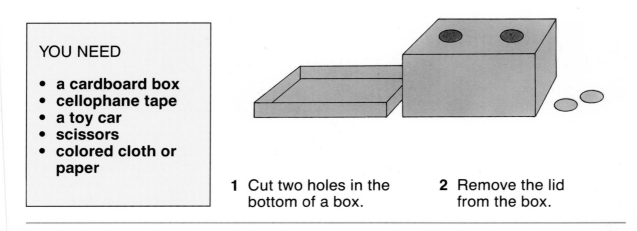

1 Cut two holes in the bottom of a box.

2 Remove the lid from the box.

3 Tape a filter over one of the holes.
4 Place the toy car on the colored cloth or paper.

5 Place the box over the car with the filter side up.
6 Look through the hole. How has the color of the car and cloth changed?

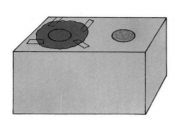
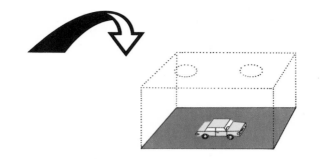

MIXING COLORED LIGHT

1 Work with a friend.
2 Use cellophane tape to fasten a red filter to one flashlight and a green filter to the other.

3 Tape the white paper to the wall. Darken the room.

4 Shine the red light onto the paper. At the same time, shine the green light onto the spot where the red light is.

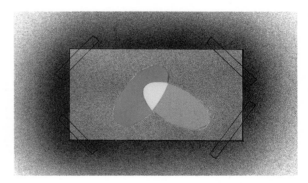

5 If the filters are good, you should see a yellow patch where the light beams overlap.
6 Try the filters in different combinations.
7 Record your results.

TEST YOURSELF

1. What color do you get when you mix red and green light?
2. If you look at a white car through a green filter, what color does it seem to be? Explain your answer.

LIGHT AND GLASS

Glass is one of the most transparent substances that we commonly use. People have known how to make glass for about 4,500 years, but it was only recently that we discovered how to make really flat glass.

All of the light spectrum passes through glass, except for ultraviolet and infrared, which humans cannot see. Glass is opaque to ultraviolet light. Infrared can only pass through at right angles to the glass.

Even the best glass is not completely transparent. Some of the light that shines on a window is scattered, making a reflection. On a cloudy or dark day, you can see the room reflected more clearly than you can see outside. That is because more light is bouncing off the glass inside than is coming through from outside.

Infrared (heat) rays from the sun pass through glass only at right angles. So, they get trapped inside until they manage to hit the glass at the correct angle to escape. This heats the air inside the greenhouse.

ACTIVITIES

LOOKING AT WINDOW GLASS

1 Look out the window on a cloudy day.
2 Switch off the room lights.
3 Stand directly in front of the glass. What do you see?
4 Now switch the room lights on again.
5 Look out the window again. Is there any change in what you can see?

LOOKING AT PLATE GLASS

YOU NEED
- **cellophane tape**
- **a small sheet of glass**
- **black and white paper**
- **aluminum foil**
- **a flashlight**
- **scissors**

1 Carefully tape all around the edge of the glass so that you will not cut yourself if it has a sharp edge.
2 Look through the glass and slowly turn it until it is at an angle toward you. What happens?
3 Hold a sheet of white paper behind the glass. What can you see?
4 Try using black paper or aluminum foil in place of the white paper. What makes the best mirror?

WARNING: Be careful with glass!

TEST YOURSELF

1. Name three solid, transparent substances.
2. What type of light cannot pass through glass?
3. Explain how you would turn a sheet of clear glass into a mirror.

MIRRORS AND SYMMETRY

We usually think of a mirror as a piece of glass with a silver backing, but the word mirror means any surface that is smooth and can reflect images. Look in the mirror and you see your reflection. That is the image and you are the object. Your image is exactly like you, except that it is reversed—in other words, your right hand is your image's left hand. The sort of mirror that you will mostly see is flat and called a plane mirror.

You can use a plane mirror to find out if things are symmetrical. An object is sym-

Left *This scarlet tiger moth is bilaterally symmetrical.*

Right *This edible sea urchin is radially symmetrical.*

metrical if its parts match on either side of a straight line (bilateral symmetry) or surrounding a midpoint (radial symmetry).

An elephant is bilaterally symmetrical. If you drew a line from the elephant's trunk to the tail, it would match on both sides of the line. A sea urchin is round and radially symmetrical.

ACTIVITIES

YOU NEED

- **large and small plane mirrors**
- **paper**
- **pencil**
- **paint and paintbrush**

LOOKING IN A MIRROR

1 Look at the reflection or image of your face in a mirror.
2 Wink your right eye. Which eye winked in your image?
3 Wave your left hand. Which hand waved back at you?
4 Try with your right hand.

5 Write your name in capital letters on a sheet of paper.

6 Hold it up to the mirror. How many of the letter images look "correct" and how many look "wrong"?

7 Now try to write your name so it can be read correctly in a mirror.

8 This is called mirror writing.

9 Many vehicles have signs painted on the front in mirror writing.

Why do you think these vehicles have mirror-writing signs?

BILATERAL SYMMETRY

1 Write down the capital letter A.

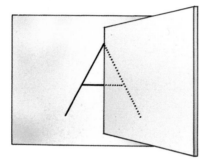

2 Place a mirror upright on the A to cut it in half.

3 Notice that the letter is still perfect. It is bilaterally symmetrical.

4 Check all the letters of the alphabet this way.

5 Some words are bilaterally symmetrical. Try to find some.

6 Fold a sheet of paper in half and crease it along the fold.

7 Open the paper.

8 Drop some paint on one side of the crease in the paper.

9 Fold the paper and press the paint.

10 Open the paper again. Notice how the shapes match on either side of the crease.

11 Hold a mirror upright along the crease. Is the shape bilaterally symmetrical?

12 Test pictures of animals in this way. See how many you can find that are bilaterally symmetrical.

TEST YOURSELF

1. What is a flat mirror called?
2. Write down three bilaterally symmetrical letters. Explain how you would check this.
3. Are you bilaterally symmetrical?

REFLECTIONS

When light hits a shiny opaque surface it is reflected or bounced off. A ray of light that hits a mirror shines through the transparent glass. Then it reaches the shiny silver backing and bounces back through the glass. It comes back out as a ray of light.

You already know that light is scattered from an object. If the scattered light hits a mirror and bounces back into your eyes, your brain would tell you that you can see the object in the mirror. It tells you that you are looking at the image of the object. If the mirror is flat, the image seems to be as far behind the mirror as the object is in front.

Below *A diagram to show reflection in a plane mirror. Notice the image seems as far behind the mirror as the object is in front.*

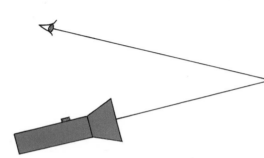

Left *The effects in a "Hall of Mirrors" are created by mirrors made of concave and convex sections. The convex sections make the boy look shorter and fatter, and the concave sections stretch him out and sometimes turn him upside down.*

ACTIVITY

IMAGES IN A MIRROR

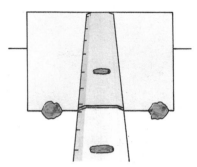

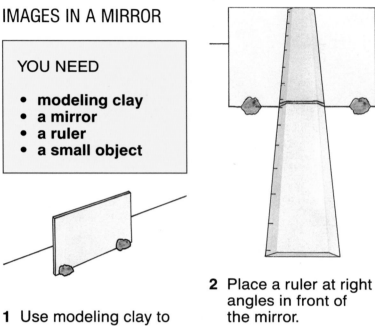

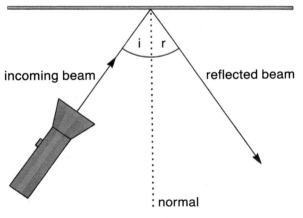

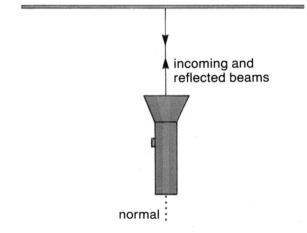

1 Use modeling clay to stand a mirror upright on a table.

2 Place a ruler at right angles in front of the mirror.

3 Look in the mirror. Look for the image of the ruler.

4 Place a lump of modeling clay on the ruler.

5 Look into the mirror. How far behind the mirror does the clay seem to be?

6 Try your experiment again. Place the object in different positions.

There are two things that can happen when a ray of light hits a flat mirror. The first is shown in the diagram:

incoming beam

reflected beam

i : r

: normal

The ray of light from the flashlight hits the mirror at an angle called i (the angle of incidence). It bounces back, as a ball would, at an angle called r (the angle of reflection). If you measure the angles i and r with a protractor, you will find that they are the same.

The second rule is that when the ray of light hits the mirror at right angles, it bounces straight back. This angle is unique and is called the "normal."

incoming and reflected beams

normal :

ACTIVITY

REFLECTIONS IN A PLANE MIRROR

YOU NEED	
• scissors	• pencil
• black paper	• white paper
• flashlight	• mirror
• cellophane tape	• modeling clay
	• ruler
	• protractor

1 Cut a piece of black paper so that it fits over the front of the flashlight.

2 Cut a slit in the black paper.

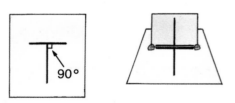

3 Tape the paper over the front of the flashlight.

4 Use a pencil to draw a large T on the sheet of white paper.

5 Place the mirror, facing the letter, at the base of the letter T.

6 Use clay to hold the mirror in place.

7 Darken the room.

8 Stand slightly to one side of the mirror.

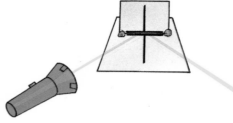

9 Hold your flashlight so that the ray of light strikes the mirror where the pencil line touches it.

10 Note what happens to the light ray.

11 Draw along the rays of light with a ruler. Draw arrows on your lines to show the direction the light travels.

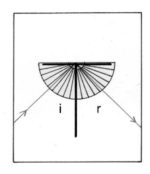

12 You have drawn the angle of incidence and the angle of reflection.

13 Measure both angles with your protractor. Are they equal?

14 Move the flashlight to alter the angle of incidence. Repeat the experiment.

TEST YOURSELF

1. If you put an object 2 inches in front of a flat mirror, how far behind the mirror does the image seem to be?
2. What is the name of the angle at which light hits a mirror?
3. What is the normal?

BOUNCING LIGHT

You know how a plane mirror can reflect light and create an image. If you stand two mirrors facing each other, the image from the first mirror is reflected in the second. You can see another image. Some very interesting visual effects can be created by using two or more mirrors. This is the basis of many magic tricks. Kaleidoscopes use mirrors to bounce light to each other and make beautiful, symmetrical patterns. If the object used inside the kaleidoscope is constantly moved, an almost endless number of patterns can be made.

Mirrors can also be used to bounce light around corners. Many special effects at laser-light shows are created with mirrors. A laser sends out a narrow, but very strong, beam of light. This can be reflected off mirrors set far apart, so that the effects can be seen by a large audience.

An instrument using mirrors to see around corners is called a periscope. It was very effective in wartime, when someone in a submarine or trench could see what was going on above without being seen.

Laser beams are bounced off mirrors to create the patterns in this display.

The greatest invention using bouncing light is fiber optics. This technology uses very fine, flexible cables that have total internal reflection. This means that light shone into one end of the fiber will bounce from side to side and not shine out until it reaches the end. Because no light is lost from the side of the fiber, all the light put

Each fiber-optic filament in this large bundle carries light along to the end, without losing any on the way.

in at one end will come out at the other. Fiber optics have many uses. For example, they allow doctors to see inside a patient's body.

ACTIVITIES

MAKING A PERISCOPE

YOU NEED

- 2 mirrors
- scissors
- a ruler
- a balsa wood cube cut in half diagonally
- strong cardboard, at least 20 inches long
- cellophane tape
- glue

1 Tape a mirror to each diagonally cut surface of the balsa wood block.

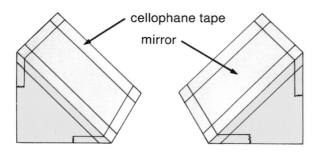

cellophane tape

mirror

2 Cut two strips of cardboard, each 20 inches long and as wide as the blocks.
3 Tape the cardboard to the sides of the blocks.

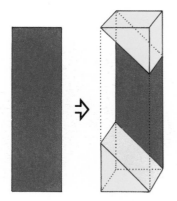

4 Cut two more strips 15 inches long and as wide as the blocks.

5 Tape one strip to the bottom of each block so that you can see the mirrors.

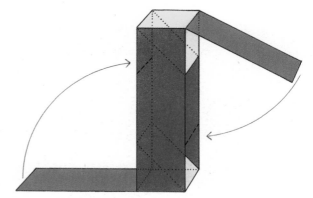

6 Use tape to strengthen the corners of the tube you have formed.
7 You now have a periscope with a block and mirror at each end.

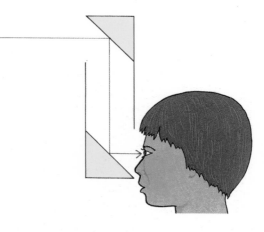

8 Use it to look around corners and in places too high for you to see.

TEST YOURSELF

1. What happens to the number of images when two mirrors are gradually turned to face each other?
2. Explain how a periscope helps a submarine captain to see what is happening above the surface of the water.

CURVED MIRRORS

Mirrors do not have to be flat—they can be curved. If a mirror is curved inward like a bowl, it is concave. If it is curved outward like a ball, it is convex. These curved mirrors reflect light in a different way from flat mirrors. The images formed in curved mirrors look different from those in flat mirrors.

Convex mirrors make the image seem small. This means that you can see more in a convex mirror than you can in a plane mirror of the same size. A convex mirror is useful for showing what is behind you. This is why the rearview and sideview mirrors in a car or truck are usually convex. The driver can see the car behind, as well as a large section of the road.

Above *You can see much more of the road behind with a convex driving mirror.*

This dentist is using a concave mirror to check the boy's teeth.

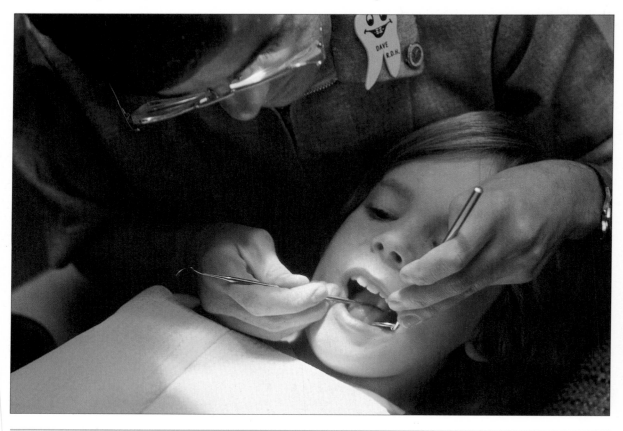

Concave mirrors make the image seem large, but only when held close. If you move away from a concave mirror, your image turns upside down. Dentists use them to look at your teeth to check for cavities.

Three hundred years ago, Sir Isaac Newton was the first person to use a concave mirror in a reflecting telescope. The largest today is on Mount Semirodriki in the Caucasus Mountains of the Soviet Union. It is almost 20 feet in diameter.

ACTIVITY

YOU NEED

- **a small plane mirror**
- **several shiny spoons**

1 Look into the small mirror and notice how large your eye's image is.
2 Look at a spoon to see which side is concave and which side is convex.
3 Look into the bowl of the spoon.

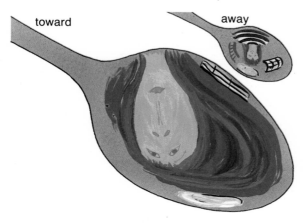

4 What happens when you move the bowl of the spoon toward your eye?

5 Does the image appear larger or smaller than in the mirror?
6 What happens when you move the spoon away from your eye?
7 Look into the back of the spoon.

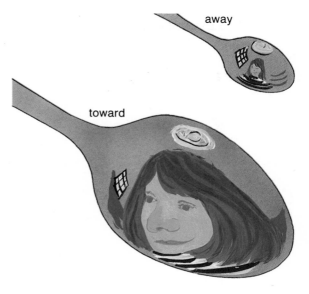

8   Is the image larger or smaller?
9   What happens to the image when you move the spoon away from your eye?
10 Compare several different spoons. Is the effect the same as before?

TEST YOURSELF

1. What does a convex mirror do to the image of an object?
2. Name one use for a convex mirror.
3. Name two uses for a concave mirror.

REFRACTION OF LIGHT

Have you ever noticed that if you put your arm in water and look down at it, your arm seems to bend where it touches the water. You also might have seen that something underwater often looks much closer than it really is. This is because light can be bent by water and other substances, such as glass. This light-bending is called refraction. It happens when light passes from one transparent substance to another, such as from air to water.

Air is not very dense—in other words, the air particles are not very close together, which is why it is a gas. Light can travel quite quickly through air. Water is much denser—its particles are closer together, which is why it is liquid. It is harder for light to travel through water, so it moves more slowly. Glass is even more dense, since it is solid. Light travels more slowly through glass than it does through water.

Imagine a light beam traveling through the air and hitting a block of glass at an

The straw looks bent, due to refraction.

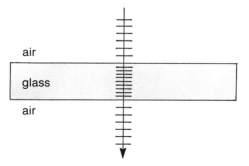

angle. The light slows down when it hits the glass and continues to travel at the lower speed through the glass block. When the light reaches the air on the other side of the block, the light beam exits at an angle.

Why does light bend as it enters and exits the glass block? The light wave that reaches the glass first is immediately slowed down, while the other light waves in the beam continue to travel at their speed in air. One by one, the light waves reach the glass and are slowed down. This makes the light beam bend toward the glass.

When the beam reaches the other side of the glass block, the leading wave suddenly

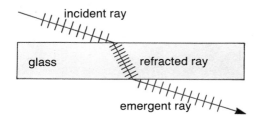

speeds up as it hits the air. The waves in the beam speed up one by one, as they reach the air. This causes the light beam to bend away from the glass.

ACTIVITY

1 Put the block of glass on the page of a book.

light **trave**ls
very **slowl**y
thro**ugh g**lass

2 Look at the print through the glass block. What do you notice?
3 Try the block in different positions.
4 Make a slit in black paper to tape over your flashlight.
5 Place the block of glass on the sheet of white paper.
6 Darken the room.
7 Hold the flashlight so that a ray of light strikes the side of the glass block at an angle of about 60°.
8 Note what happens to the light ray.
9 Draw around the block. Mark where the light ray goes in (incident) and comes out the other side (emergent).

10 Take away the block. On the paper, mark the position of the beam in the glass block.
11 Repeat your experiment, using another piece of paper and a different angle for your light ray.

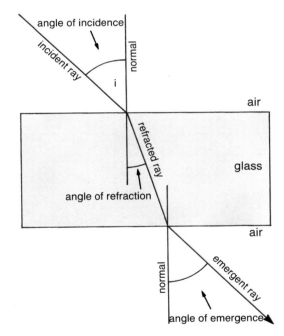

PRISMS AND LENSES

You have found out that light can be bent if it goes from one transparent substance to another. In the last chapter, you saw what happens if a rectangular block is used. You can also use triangular prisms, like the one that you used on page 13, to get some interesting refraction effects.

If a ray of light strikes a triangular glass prism at an angle other than 90°, the light is refracted as before—toward the normal. When the light reaches the other side of the prism, it refracts away from the normal, just as it did for the rectangular block.

If two prisms are put together base to base, and a ray of light is shone on both, the two beams of light converge (meet) on the other side of the prisms. The point at which they converge is called the focus.

If you put the two prisms the other way around, the effect is different; the two beams of light diverge (do not meet).

Remember, when light passes through a triangular prism, it is always bent toward the base of the prism.

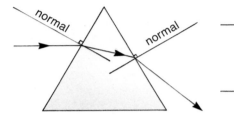

A single prism deflects the light beam toward its base.

Two prisms base-to-base converge the light beams.

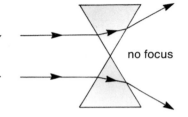

Two prisms apex-to-apex diverge the light beams.

ACTIVITY

YOU NEED

- **black paper**
- **scissors**
- **cellophane tape**
- **a flashlight**
- **two triangular glass prisms**
- **sheet of white paper**

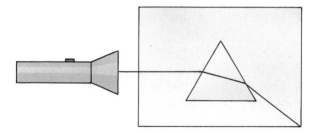

1 Use the black paper to make a slit for your flashlight.
2 Place a prism on the white paper.
3 Darken the room.
4 Hold the flashlight so the light ray strikes the side of the prism at an angle. Try not to make a spectrum.

5 Draw around the prism and mark the positions of the incident and emergent rays of light.
6 Mark the position of the ray within the block.
7 Repeat your experiment, using a new piece of paper and a different angle of incidence.

8 Take the slit from the flashlight.
9 Place the two prisms base to base.
10 Shine your flashlight close to both prisms.
11 What happens to the beam of light? Draw what you see.
12 Try the light close to and far from the prisms. Draw what you see.
13 Repeat your experiment with the two prisms joined point to point. How do the results differ?

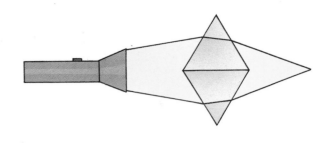

THE SHAPE OF A LENS

Glass lenses can be made in many shapes. We shall consider two—the double convex (or biconvex) and the double concave (or biconcave).

A biconvex lens is somewhat like two prisms placed base to base, and works in a similar way (see page 34). The rays of light passing through the lens all meet at a focus.

The distance of the focus from the lens depends on the curvature—that is, how thick the lens is. The thicker it is, the nearer the focus is to the lens. The smaller the curvature, the farther the focus is from the lens.

A concave lens is like two prisms placed point to point. The rays of light shining through the lens do not meet on the other side. In other words, there is no focus.

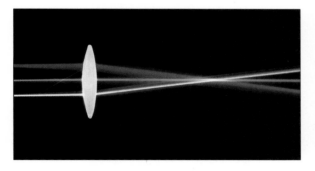

A double convex (biconvex) lens brings light beams to a focus.

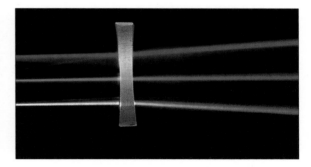

A double concave (biconcave) lens causes light beams to diverge.

TEST YOURSELF

1. How does a triangular prism refract light?
2. What happens to a beam of light that is shone onto two prisms placed base to base?
3. What happens to a beam of light that is shone onto two prisms placed point to point?

OUR EYES

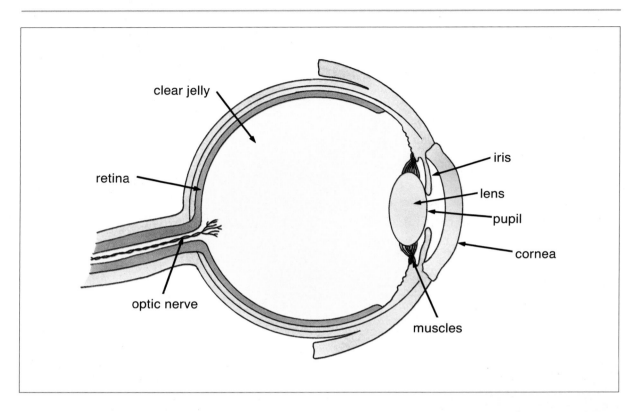

clear jelly

retina

optic nerve

iris

lens

pupil

cornea

muscles

Most animals can see what we know as visible light. Some can see light outside our visible spectrum but many cannot see color. We see through our eyes, where light is focused onto the light-sensitive area called the retina.

Light rays come from objects that you are looking at. The light is refracted by the curved cornea, the lens, and the jelly-like substance within the eyeball.

Muscles are attached to the lens of the eye. They pull on it, changing its shape so that it focuses incoming light rays onto the retina. The lens causes the image on the retina to be upside down, but the brain corrects it, so you see things right way up.

The amount of light that reaches the retina is controlled by the iris (the colored part). The iris has muscles that get longer if

A diagram to show the main features of the eye. The optic nerve carries the information to the brain, which interprets it as sight.

the light is bright, or shorter if it is dim. The hole in the middle of the iris is called the pupil. It gets bigger when the iris muscles shorten and smaller when they lengthen. When the pupil is big, much light can enter the eye.

The retina contains cells that enable us to see color. There are two types of cells. The rod-shaped cells help us to see black, white, and gray and are used for night vision. The cone-shaped cells are for strong light. There are three kinds of cones—one absorbs blue light, one absorbs red light, and one absorbs green light. They work together so we see all the spectrum colors.

ACTIVITY

YOU NEED

- **a large mirror**

1 Look into the mirror. Notice the shape of your eyes.
2 What color is the iris?
3 Look at your friend's eyes from the side. Notice how the iris bulges out.
4 Look at your eyebrows and eyelashes. They prevent moisture and dust from entering your eyes.

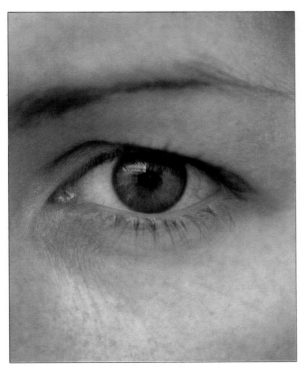

5 Watch your friend blink his or her eyes. Notice how the eyelids move.
6 Close one eye. Notice the position of your eyelid over your closed eye.
7 Look for your tearducts in the corners of your eyes, near your nose.

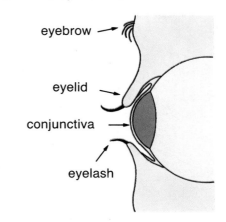

8 Try yawning—this makes your eyes water. Try yawning with your eyes open, and see your tearducts work.
9 Look at the whites of your eyes. Can you see the tiny blood vessels? Cover your eyes for 5 seconds.
10 Uncover your eyes quickly and notice how the pupils change.
11 Look out the window for 5 seconds.
12 Look quickly back at the mirror. How do the pupils change?
13 Draw your eyes. Label your drawing.
14 Make a survey of the eye colors of the students in your class. Draw a bar graph to show the results. Which color is most common?

TEST YOURSELF

1. What is the light-sensitive layer of the eye called?
2. What controls the amount of light entering the eye?
3. Why do you think that you blink your eyes so often?

COMMON EYE PROBLEMS

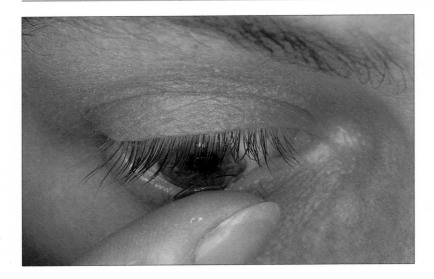

This person is putting in a hard contact lens. The lens and the finger must be very clean. The lens is washed with a special solution, then carefully placed over the eye.

You may know people who wear glasses or contact lenses. Perhaps you wear glasses or contacts yourself. If you do, it is probably because your eyes cannot focus properly. There are three main reasons why this happens.

Nearsighted people either have eyeballs that are too long, or lenses of the eye that are too thick. This refracts the light too much when it enters the eye and the image is focused short of the retina. The picture is blurred on the retina. Concave lenses are used to focus objects that are far away. Glasses for nearsightedness make a person's eyes look smaller.

Farsighted people either have short eye-

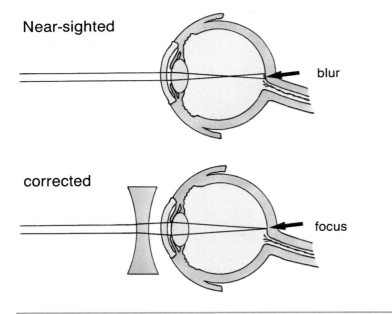

Near-sighted

blur

corrected

focus

Above A diagram to show where the light from an object focuses in a nearsighted eye.

Below A diagram to show how nearsightedness can be corrected, using a concave lens.

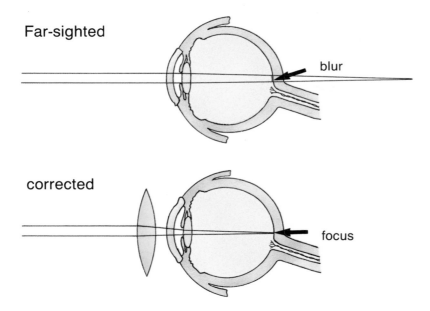

Far-sighted

blur

corrected

focus

Above *A diagram to show where the light from an object focuses in a farsighted eye.*

Below *A diagram to show how farsightedness can be corrected, using a convex lens.*

balls, or lenses that are too thin. The light does not get refracted enough and the image is focused behind the retina. The picture is again blurred on the retina. Convex lenses are used to correct farsightedness, especially when a person is reading. Glasses for farsightedness make eyes look larger.

It is very common for middle-aged and older people to be farsighted, because the lenses of the eye start to harden and cannot change shape easily. Most twelve-year-olds can focus on an object 4 inches from the eye, while many forty-year-olds are not able to focus on an object any closer than 10 inches from the eye.

Some people are astigmatic. This means that the cornea does not curve properly. The eye cannot focus on vertical and horizontal objects at the same time. A special lens has to be used to correct astigmatism. This lens corrects the light in one direction. The person can then concentrate on the horizontal objects, while the lens brings the vertical objects into focus.

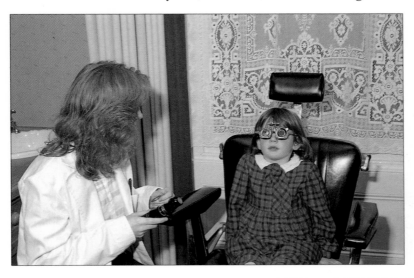

This little girl is at the optician, having her eyes tested. The special spectacles are for holding different lenses and for measurements to be made.

OPTICAL ILLUSIONS

You know that when you see something, an image forms on your retina. The light-sensitive cells send messages (called nerve impulses) to your brain. The brain decodes the messages and tells you what you are looking at, what color it is, and how far away it is. You depend not only on your eyes, but also your brain, to be able to see things properly.

Your two eyes see a slightly different picture of an object. The brain's job is to overlap the images so that you see one image. The amount of overlap is linked to our ability to judge distance by eye.

Sometimes, you can trick your eyes with pictures that have more than one interpretation. The brain can get confused, because one eye sees the picture in one way and the other eye sees it slightly differently. This is especially true if the picture is close to your face. This type of visual trick is called an optical illusion.

There is another kind of optical illusion, where images can be shown very quickly, one after the other. The brain runs all the pictures together, so that the person watching sees continuous movement. This is what happens when you watch a movie or television. Television works by showing hundreds of colored lines, very quickly. The brain "blends" the lines together and the viewer sees a screen full of moving pictures.

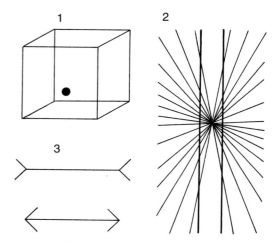

1 Is the dot at the front or back of the cube?
2 Are the heavy lines straight or curved?
3 Are the lines the same length?

Left *Moving pictures are made up of thousands of photographs taken at very close time intervals, which are run through a projector very quickly.*

ACTIVITIES

MAKING MOVING PICTURES

> **YOU NEED**
> - **thick card-board**
> - **scissors**
> - **crayons**
> - **cellophane tape**
> - **pencil**
> - **notebook**

1 Cut out a 3 inch × 3 inch square of cardboard.

2 Draw a fish in the middle of the square. Color the fish.

3 Draw a net centered on the back of the card. Color the net black.

4 Tape the pencil to the card.

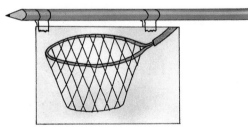

5 Spin the pencil between your hands, as fast as you can.

6 What do you see on the card?

7 Draw, at the top corner of each page of the notebook, the various stages of a high jump.

8 Start with the run-up, so the figure is moving its legs, then taking off, getting higher, eventually clearing the bar and landing.

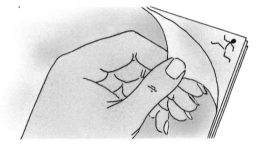

9 Use your thumb to flip through the pages to see the action. Note that if the pictures appear jerky you probably need to draw more pictures.

10 Make other cartoons, using the same technique.

TEST YOURSELF

1. What does your brain receive from the light-sensitive cells in your eyes?

2. Your two eyes see slightly different images. How do you manage to see only one?

PHOTOGRAPHY

Before photography was invented, pictures were seen on a camera obscura. Here, light passed through a lens and an image was seen on a ground glass screen. No permanent record could be kept of the image. An early camera was like the camera obscura. It consisted of a lens at one end to let in the light. The light fell onto either light-sensitive paper or a light-sensitive metal plate inside the box.

In 1826, the Frenchman Joseph Nicéphore Niepce made the first photograph. In 1835, the Englishman W.H. Fox Talbot was the first to use light-sensitive paper.

Left A negative photographic image. This positive image (right) has been developed from the negative. Notice the reversing of black and white.

The Frenchman, L.J.M. Daguerre, who worked with Niepce, used a copper plate coated with a light-sensitive silver compound.

When light strikes the light-sensitive compound, the silver turns from white to black. If a scene is photographed, the lighter parts in the scene make the silver blacker. The dark parts have little light, so the silver stays white or turns gray. This means that the picture created on the light-sensitive plate has its black and white colors reversed. It is called a negative. Today, the negative is on plastic. To develop a photograph, the negative is fixed. This means putting it in chemical baths that dissolve the white parts of the silver and leave the darker areas behind. Fixing must be done in the dark, so that no more silver is turned

black. After the negative is fixed, light is shone through it onto a piece of light-sensitive paper. The parts where the silver is still on the film will not let the light through, so these areas are white or pale on the paper.

Black and white on the negative are now reversed—just as they were in the original scene. The paper is fixed and washed, becoming a photograph. A more complicated process is used for color pictures.

ACTIVITY

MAKING A PINHOLE CAMERA

YOU NEED

- **a hammer and nail**
- **an empty can**
- **scissors**
- **aluminum foil**
- **cellophane tape**
- **a pin**
- **waxed paper**
- **rubber bands**

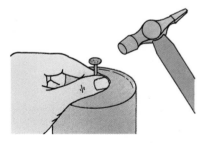

1 Use a hammer and nail to make a small hole in the base of the can.

2 Cut out a circle of foil. Tape the foil firmly to the bottom of the can.
3 Make a small hole in the foil with a pin, in line with the hole in the bottom of the can.
4 Stretch a sheet of waxed paper tightly over the open end of the can.
5 Make sure the surface is smooth.

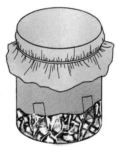

6 Use the rubber band to hold the paper in place. The waxed paper serves as the screen.

7 Darken the room.
8 Hold your can so that the pinhole points toward the window and the screen points toward you. What can you see on the screen?

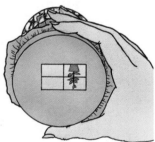

9 Notice that the picture is upside down. This is the way a camera works except that a pinhole is used instead of a lens.

TEST YOURSELF

1. Describe a camera obscura.
2. Explain how a negative is made.
3. Why do you think that the image is upside down in a pinhole camera?

LIGHT AS ENERGY

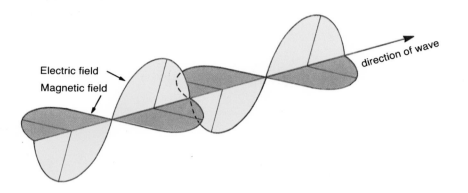

Electric field
Magnetic field
direction of wave

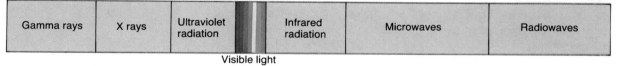

Short wavelength

Long wavelength

| Gamma rays | X rays | Ultraviolet radiation | | Infrared radiation | Microwaves | Radiowaves |

Visible light

You have been learning about visible light, and its properties. In addition to visible light there are other types of rays. When you stand in sunlight, you are affected by some of these rays. You can feel the infrared rays warming you. The sunlight also contains ultraviolet light, which will tan your skin. You cannot see infrared, or ultraviolet, so they are not part of our visible spectrum. Visible, infrared, and ultraviolet light are part of the electromagnetic spectrum. This spectrum also contains the long, medium, and short waves of radio and television and the shorter waves of radar. Then come the shorter waves of infrared, visible light, ultraviolet, and X rays.

X rays are so short that they pass through flesh—so we can say that flesh is transparent to X rays. Bones are denser than flesh. X rays cannot pass through bones, so X-ray photographs can show the condition of the bones in a body. Because

The electromagnetic spectrum stretches from gamma rays to radio waves. Our visible light spectrum is only a tiny part.

excessive exposure to X rays can harm the body, doctors limit the use of X rays.

Gamma rays are shorter than X rays. They are dangerous and radioactive. The cosmic rays from the sun are the shortest, and they can pass through buildings. We have seen how visible light can cause chemical reactions, such as in photography. It also enables green plants to make their own food.

Electricity can be made from sunlight. A special cell is made from two different metals dipped in a solution that can conduct electricity. Light is shone on this cell, and causes an electric current to flow. The brighter the light, the more current flows. This is how solar cells work. Sunlight is our ultimate source of energy.

Left *The turnip usually needs to be underground all winter before it will flower. Using the energy from the special lights in this greenhouse, it can flower in three weeks.*

Right *This calculator is run by solar cells, which are batteries powered by the sun's light energy.*

TEST YOURSELF

1. What rays give heat in the electromagnetic spectrum?
2. Name three rays in the electromagnetic spectrum that we cannot see.
3. How are X rays used?

GLOSSARY

Camera obscura   A dark box into which light comes through a small hole or convex lens to form an image on paper or ground glass.

Camouflage   The art of disguise or concealment. It comes from a French word meaning to conceal something.

Color   This is caused by a narrow band of wavelengths called the light spectrum. The order of the spectrum is red, orange, yellow, green, blue, indigo, and violet.

Color vision   The ability to see color.

Concave   Curved in like the bowl of a spoon.

Conjunctiva   The membrane that covers the front of the eyeball inside the eyelids. It is very sensitive and has many tiny blood vessels.

Convergent   Rays of light that meet at one point—the focus.

Convex   Curved out, like the back of a spoon. Convex is the opposite of concave.

Cornea   The clear part of the eyeball that lets in light.

Cosmic rays   Shortwave rays.

Divergent   Rays of light that go away from each other. Divergent is the opposite of convergent.

Energy   The power needed to do work.

Focus   The point at which rays meet after they have been reflected. An image looks clear when it is in focus.

Horizon   The line at which the earth and sky seem to meet.

Infrared rays   Invisible rays that give heat.

Iris   This controls the amount of light entering the eye. By contracting (getting smaller) it makes the pupil smaller and allows less light in. The iris gives the eye its color.

Kaleidoscope   A tube through which can be seen symmetrical patterns caused by reflections from mirrors.

Membrane   A very thin layer.

Mirror   A polished surface that reflects light to form an image.

Neon light   A light formed when electricity is passed through a sealed low-pressure tube containing neon gas.

Opaque   Light-blocking. Light does not shine through opaque objects.

Optic nerve   A small tube coming from the brain. It connects to the retina at the blind spot.

Periscope   An instrument that has two mirrors, that bounce light so that a person can see things above. (It is used in trenches and submarines to see above the surface.)

Photograph   A picture made when light falls onto a special film.

Pupil   The round opening in the center of the iris. Light enters the eye through the pupil.

Rainbow   An arch of colors formed by sunlight passing through raindrops. The order of colors is the same as the light spectrum—red, orange, yellow, green, blue, indigo, and violet.

Reflection   This is a wave or ray that bounces off something. It is also another name for the image of an object seen in a mirror.

Refraction   The bending that takes place when a ray of light passes at any angle other than at right angles from the surface of one medium to another.

Retina   Thin layer of light-sensitive cells that lines the inside of the eye.

Silhouette   Appearance of a person or object seen against the light so that only the outline is visible.

Symmetry Where parts match exactly on either side of a straight line.

Translucent Something that lets some light through so that objects placed behind can be seen faintly.

Transparent Light-transmitting. Light shines through transparent substances. Objects placed behind transparent substances can be clearly seen.

Ultraviolet rays Invisible rays that cause skin to tan and burn.

Vitreous body A transparent, jelly-like substance that fills the eyeball behind the lens, giving the eyeball its shape.

White light Light that contains all the colors in the visible spectrum; that is red, orange, yellow, green, blue, indigo, and violet.

X Rays Invisible rays that can be used to photograph bones.

Books to Read

How Did We Find Out about the Speed of Light, Isaac Asimov (Walker, 1986)

Fiber Optics, Charlene W. Billings (Dodd, Mead, 1986)

The Penetrating Beam, Edith Levin (Rosen, 1978)

Light Fantastic, Philip Watson (Lothrop, 1983)

Picture Acknowledgments

The author and publishers would like to thank the following for allowing illustrations to be reproduced in this book: Chapel Studios, *cover*, 6, 10, 12, 17, 30 (above), 32, 37, 39, 40, 42, 45 (below); Jenny Hughes, 24; Oxford Scientific Films, 14, 16 (Michael Fogden), 22 (left, Gordon Maclean), 22 (right, Fredrik Ehrenstrom); © Pete Salacutos, TSW-Wick, Chicago (*cover, upper right*); © Ellen Schuster/The Image Bank (*cover, lower right*); Science Photo Library, 27, 28, 35, 38, 45 (above); ZEFA, *cover, frontispiece,* 8, 20, 30 (below). All artwork is by Jenny Hughes.

Index